The Magic of the Forest

A Tale of Kindness, Friendship and Courage

WRITTEN & PHOTOGRAPHED BY

Jacqueline Crivello

Acknowledgments

There is one thing in life of which I'm sure—we did not get here by ourselves. We've had help—whether it be at birth, throughout our lives, or celebrating our achievements. So, first of all, thank you, Mom.

I offer a very special thanks to the people in my life who helped me use my gifts for this book. I thank God for opening doors and for giving me the ability to "see" nature. Without that, I'm sure I'd not be who I am.

I'm grateful to Michael Daniels, my publishing coach and friend, who for decades has offered the greatest of encouragement; to Karen McDiarmid, who helped see these pages unfurl with her extraordinary talent; to Holly Jorgensen, a brilliant editor and trusted friend; to Greg Dunn for his color expertise; and to my Dad, Earl Niehusen, who put the camera in my hand at a very young age.

Thanks also to my children, Tony and Lindey, and to my grandchildren, Macy, Blake, Camryn, Wyatt and Vinnie. A special heartfelt thanks to my grandson, Jett Neudorff, for his curiosity. He inspired this story when he first used my binoculars to discover a close-up look at nature.

Publisher

Happy Hill Press
P.O. Box 290
Conifer, Colorado 80433
jc@happyhillpress.com
happyhillpress.com

Karen McDiarmid, Book Design
KarenMcDiarmidDesign.com

Crivello, Jacqueline
The Magic of the Forest
by Jacqueline Crivello, Evergreen, CO
Happy Hill Press © 2020

Summary: The story of a wise grandmother, a little boy with
a kind heart, and a lost Chukar Partridge's journey to find home.
The friendship of the boy and the forest animals help the little
bird find the courage he needs to keep searching.

Printed and bound March 2021
Friesens of Altona, Manitoba, Canada

ISBN 978-0-578-63856-0

Animals; Chukar Partridge / Birds / Woods / Children
Library of Congress Control Number: 2020901226

10 9 8 7 6 5 4 3

May God always guide you;
May the angels always keep you;
And may love surprise you
In beautiful and unusual places.

Jacqueline Crivello

I am Laythe.

I come from the far reaches of
the big and friendly forest.
I have a special story to share.

Since I must avoid humans,
I will only be here a short while—
just long enough to tell you this extraordinary tale.

It's the story of a little boy, his wise grandmother
and his secret forest friend.

I will stay with you throughout the whole story.

Prepare to open your mind,

your heart,

and listen well...

"If you look into the forest, the forest eyes will look back," the wise grandmother began. She knew the secrets of the forest. The little boy listened eagerly to her words.

"If you wait quietly, if you watch carefully, the secrets of the forest will reveal themselves and a special friend will come to greet you," she continued.

"First, the forest must trust you. Keep watching, little one. Keep waiting. And do the forest no harm," she whispered. "Your special forest friend will come to you, but only if you trust and believe."

And then she quickly repeated,

"You must believe."

"There's a secret friend in this whole big forest
just for me, Grandmother?"

"I DO believe! I can believe!
I can trust! But who is it?
Who could it be?
And when will he come?"

"Patience,"
Grandmother said, wistfully.
"Have patience."

"I can be patient. I can be patient and I can be still,"
said the little boy, his imagination dancing.
"I can feel it!" he exclaimed.
"Is he watching me now?"

"Please come out of the forest, secret friend.
Please come to see me," the little boy said.
The forest was quiet as it waited to
reveal his secret friend.

Meanwhile,
as the friendly forest waited
and the story unfolded...

I, Laythe,
was watching all.

The animals were listening.
They recognized the little boy's kind heart.
They wanted to help.

"I'm here! I'm here!"
squeaked Lucky the Mouse.
"I'll help!
I'll help
find the friend!"

"Pffft.
You're too small to help,"
said Fireball the Fox.

"It's me, Fireball, to the rescue!
I'll find the secret friend!
I think he's in here.
He's right here!"

"Oh, Fireball! It's not yet time—
you must be patient, too!"

"Oh, okay.
I will try," Fireball sighed.
"I promise.
I will try to be patient."

"I'll be asleep
before this story is over,"
Bumble the Bear
mumbled.

"Zzzzzzzzzzz...

unless someone has
some honey!"

Time passed and the boy
continued to watch and to wait.
He knew his secret friend would appear.
He was patient and he trusted
the winter woods.

His wise grandmother knew
his patience would
be rewarded.

One snowy morning,
the little boy looked into the forest
and saw something different.
"Oh!" he exclaimed.
"Who are you?
Are you my secret friend?"

"Grandmother! Grandmother!
My secret friend is here!
He's beautiful!
He's different from any animal
I've seen in the woods,"
said the little boy.

"You're so cute
and puffy, little bird,"
he said.
"I think I'll call you
Chubby,
my secret friend."

The little boy had never seen a bird
quite like Chubby.

This made him wonder.

"Grandmother, Chubby looks sad.
I think he's lost.
I know the forest trusts me now.
Maybe it will help me find his family."

The animals of the forest were listening.
The boy with the kind heart and
the little puffy bird needed their help.

"Who should we 'caw'?
Who should we 'caw?'"
squawked a nearby magpie.

"We'll 'caw'
everyone in the forest!"
answered a second magpie.

"We'll let them know
Chubby needs help
finding his
family!"

Ernie the Elk heard the magpies.
He wanted to help.
He bugled an alert that echoed through the trees.

The animals of the forest heard his call.

"Do you know anything
about a lost bird?"
asked Mel the Moose.

"Not I,"
answered Mort the Moose.
"But he's a bird…
can't he just fly home?"

"Can you fly, Chubby?"
asked a helpful doe.
"Some of us are thinking that
you can fly home!"

"Oh, dear. I don't know.
I usually walk,"
Chubby answered.

"But maybe...
I can try!"

"Look at me, Chubby!"
said a soaring eagle.

"Do it just like this!
Spread your wings and fly!
I can see everything from
way up here!"

Chubby tried…
      tried…
   and tried again.

"Flap your wings!
Flap really hard!
Fly above the trees
and maybe you'll find your family!"
his new friends encouraged.

Chubby tried.
And tried.
He flapped his wings.
He jumped.

"Oh, it's no use," he said.
"I'm just not good at flying."

"I'm pretty good at walking, though.
And these big red feet help me walk really fast,"
Chubby said,
as he marched across the snow,
showing his friends
how quickly he could move.

"Sorry to interrupt,"
said Bravo the Bobcat,
racing hurriedly out of the forest.

"I've been running all through these woods and
although I did not see your family,
I learned what you are, Chubby!
You are a Chukar Partridge,"
he continued.

"And you're right!
Even though Chukar Partridges are birds,
they're not so good at flying.
But they are very good at
running, walking and hopping."

Chubby considered this
new information.

He *was* good at walking. And he felt safe in this friendly forest.
His confidence was growing.

I, Laythe, looked far off into the treetops.
Chubby Chukar had no family there,
for he was a bird who did not like to fly.

But something changed in Chubby that day.
I watched it happen.

The love from his new friends
made him feel
brave and strong.

"Thank you, friends,"
Chubby said, his chest held high.
"It's time for me to walk."

"I think I can find my way now.
Thank you for making me strong
and for being my forest family!"
said Chubby.

With one last glance
at the little boy with the kind heart,
Chubby proudly and briskly
walked back into the friendly forest
from where he came.

His head was full of dreams of home.
He was ready to find his family.
His heart was filled with the love and courage
that he'd gained from his many new friends.

As the little boy with the kind heart
watched his friend walk
back into the forest,
he smiled.

"Friendship and kindness
have made that little bird so strong," he thought.
"Grandmother was right.
The magic of the forest *is* real."

The little boy with the kind heart
knew he would *always*
believe.

"Goodbye, brave little bird. Goodbye, Chubby Chukar!"